Against Bosses, Against Oligarchies:
A Conversation with Richard Rorty

Richard Rorty
Stanford University

Derek Nystrom
University of Virginia

Kent Puckett
Columbia University

Prickly Pear Pamphlets (North America)
Charlottesville, Virginia

Published by Prickly Pear Pamphlets (North America)
PO Box 136
Charlottesville, Va. 22902-0136

ISBN: 1-891754-10-6
ISSN: 1351-7961

Library of Congress Catalog Card Number: 98-066694

Printed in the United States of America

CONTENTS

INTRODUCTION

We interviewed Richard Rorty for four hours over the course of a weekend in Charlottesville. This interview is not only, we think, ideally timed, following closely several recent publications by Rorty, but captures Rorty at his most energetic. Rorty's work is well known for its geniality and measured tone, and, while our discussion remains always constructive, there appears in these pages a combative Richard Rorty familiar, perhaps, to those who have seen him in debate, but new to those who know him only from his published work.

Although the following conversation addresses many subjects—Rorty's own intellectual history, the effects of globalization, academic labor—its first motivation is the recently published *Achieving Our Country: Leftist Thought in Twentieth Century America.* That book, adapted from Rorty's 1997 Massey Lectures at Harvard University, takes as its subject the life and health of the American Left. Of course, that Left is in no way a simple or single entity and Rorty's book—part history, part diagnosis, part prescription—works to understand it both in terms of the patriotic, Whitmanesque vision that he suggests determined and consolidated its earliest course, and the particular contexts (the Vietnam War, Watergate, etc.) that seemed to allow some parts of the Left to find it "absurd for Americans to continue to take pride in their country."

Rorty begins *Achieving Our Country* (he takes the title, importantly, from the last line of James Baldwin's *The Fire Next Time*) with an account of the sources of his own Leftism, a political position that allows for and in fact demands a sense of national pride. "National pride," says Rorty, "is to countries what self-respect is to individuals: a necessary condition for self-improvement." Without patriotism, a progressive, effective, majoritarian politics is impossible and, Rorty suggests, it is the absence of that patriotism that has rendered Leftist politics enervated and without direction. With this crisis in mind, Rorty's book asks a series of basic questions: what was the Left and what are its sources? What does the Left look like today? How can the Left achieve the patriotic dignity to make a majoritarian Leftism possible once again?

Rorty's answer to the first question centers on two figures in particular: Walt Whitman and John Dewey. These thinkers did a great deal to shape "the quasi-communitarian rhetoric...at the heart of the Progressive Movement and the New Deal," and suggest for Rorty a means of thinking of America and democracy in such a way as to retain patriotism without losing one's sense of justice and one's necessary anger at injustice: "Both Dewey and Whitman viewed the United States as an opportunity to see ultimate significance in a finite, human, historical project, rather than in something eternal and nonhuman." The real secular promise of America was big enough, diverse enough, and potential enough to exceed the specific character of its weaknesses or its mistakes. That's not to say that America could do no wrong or that one should ignore wrong-doing in America's name; rather, a progressive patriotism's duty is to ensure that the "rich diversity" and promise of that America are protected and maintained.

Rorty argues that against the Whitmanesque patriot acting in the name of American potential is what he calls the spectatorial Leftist, a cultural pessimist who sees the very foundations of liberal democracy as complicit in a larger and slightly shadowy conspiracy against the powerless. Once this figure has given up all hope in the larger promise of, in this case, America, he or she becomes a passive and cynical spectator, a willfully marginal critic who sneers without suggestion and who neither cherishes principle nor can truly practice politics. This Leftist appears in a variety of contexts throughout *Achieving Our Country*, but is most clearly associated with the New Left that Rorty suggests turned away from the Old Left and against America in the sixties. Rorty's own politics grew out of the New Deal sympathies of both his family and the friends of his family, as well as the anti-Stalinist work of some of the so-called New York Intellectuals: "As a teenager, I believed every anti-Stalinist word that Sidney Hook and Lionel Trilling published in *Partisan Review*—partly, perhaps, because I had been bounced on their knees as a baby." Where Rorty's Old Leftist (Irving Howe is another example) was a public intellectual passionately committed to class politics, publishing articles in journals like *Commentary* or the *Partisan Review*, and who could "be both a fervent anti-communist and a good Leftist," the New Left (think of student anti-war protesters, Black Panthers, Tom Hayden, and Abbie Hoffman) felt that the Old Left's irrational hatred of communism underwrote the conflict in Vietnam and permitted the worst excesses of the Cold War. While Rorty agrees that the New Left did what the Old perhaps could not ("they stopped the Vietnam War"), the continuing rift between what remains of the Old Left and the New makes any majoritarian, progressive American politics difficult if not impossible.

More immediately, Rorty critiques the Cultural Left, "heirs of the New Left" who "specialize in what they call the 'politics of difference' or 'of identity' or 'of recognition'." This Left, suggests Rorty, maintains the New Left's disdain for America and thinks more about social or cultural "stigma" (in Goffman's sense) than it does about the top-down initiatives and concern for class and money that characterizes his Old Left progressive politics. These are primarily academic intellectuals (Rorty might name Andrew Ross or Fredric Jameson, for example) whose "longing for total revolution" and belief in the deep corruption of the Western tradition make a reformist politics suspect in theory and impossible in practice. While Rorty grants that this Cultural Left has reduced the amount of sadism and cruelty that the less powerful need experience and "has made America a far more civilized society than it was thirty years ago," its inability to address practically issues of class and labor has removed the Left from areas where political action could do the most good. In other words, when specific instances of economic injustice and unfair labor practices are replaced with totalizing concepts like "late capitalism" and "ideology," the Cultural Left find themselves to be practically powerless, but comfortable with the idea that they, at least, know better. "Theorists of the Left think that dissolving political agents into plays of differential subjectivity, or political initiatives into pursuits of Lacan's impossible object of desire, helps to subvert the established order." Rorty believes they are wrong. Rorty recommends finally that the separation between the Old and New Left, a rift built on conflicts decades old, must be overcome, and that the spectatorial Cultural Left must return to the messy, contingent business of progressive politics. In fact, Rorty argues, the good moral work done by the Cultural Left, work that made the lives of the less powerful better and more humane, may be undone by this Left's inability to challenge the right's largely successful and continuing economic onslaught. While the Left has worked, willfully it seems, to imagine itself as part of some minority, Rorty warns, the Right has, without opposition, captured and captivated the majority. And, if a Reformist Left is to have anything to do with the achievement of America, it isn't enough to watch politics; they must be practiced and practiced progressively.

∾

Some of the arguments put forth in *Achieving Our Country* are controversial rejoinders to positions held by many of Rorty's fellow academic Leftists—indeed, to some, they may seem almost willfully contrarian. Yet this is not an unfamiliar position for Rorty. For prior to his recent fame as a Leftist commentator (a renown which grants him the curious honor of having George Will devote an entire *Newsweek* column to attacking his latest book), Rorty was well known as an iconoclastic philosopher who challenged the precepts of his own discipline. Here, we would like to offer a brief sketch of Rorty's ideas for readers who may not be familiar with some of his important earlier work.

Rorty first came to the attention of readers outside of American philosophy departments in 1979, with the publication of *Philosophy and the Mirror of Nature*. The book was a sustained, thorough-going critique of the dominant analytic mode of philosophy practiced by most English and American philosophers. However, what was most compelling about this critique for the book's more general audience was its concomitant deconstruction of the larger "Cartesian-Kantian" tradition of thought which seeks out absolute, transcendental "foundations" for our knowledge of the world. This tradition, Rorty writes, is concerned primarily with "underwrit[ing] or debunk[ing] claims to knowledge made by science, morality, art, or religion" through an examination of the "grounds" upon which these disciplines make their knowledge-claims (3). He surveys the historical development of this philosophical tradition, and argues that while this project was important in helping to establish the secular intellectual culture of the Enlightenment, it is one which may have outlived its usefulness. However, Rorty does not make this argument by claiming that philosophy's conception of itself (as a meta-discipline which inspects the foundations of the knowledge-claims made by other disciplines) is one which somehow misconstrues its "real" role, or that this quest for epistemological foundations misunderstands the "true nature" of knowledge-claims. Instead, he proposes, we should stop worrying about the "real role" of such activities and the "true nature" of their objects of study in the first place.

Following Wittgenstein, Rorty contends that philosophy has conceived of its mission in this way because it has been held "captive" by "the picture...of the mind as a great mirror, containing various representations—some accurate, some not—and capable of being studied by pure, non-empirical methods" (12). As a way of getting out from under this picture, he suggests, as Wittgenstein did, that we view our ways of describing and explaining the world as "tools" which help us get along in that world, rather than as representations of the world which could be said to be more or less correct. Here, Rorty is talking about all sorts of linguistic practices—scientific claims, mundane observations, and so on. For example, where the traditional philosopher would describe Newton's claim that force equals mass times acceleration ($f=ma$) as true because it offers an accurate picture of the world—and thus Corresponds with Reality—Rorty asks us to view

Newton's formula as true because it provides us with an effective tool for accomplishing certain tasks in the world (such as successfully predicting force). Again, it is important to note that Rorty does not claim that "there is no such thing as truth" or, for that matter, that "there is no such thing as the outside world," but only that the question "Does this description of the world accurately correspond to what it describes?" is one which we may want to stop asking. Similarly, he does not claim that the "correspondence theory of truth" fails to grasp the true, Wittgensteinian-tool-like way language really works, only that Wittgenstein's model may be a more useful way of thinking about language for our present purposes.

In suggesting that we change our philosophical conversations, Rorty explicitly aligns himself with the tradition of American pragmatism inaugurated by William James and John Dewey a century ago. Furthermore, as he noted in his 1982 collection of essays, *Consequences of Pragmatism*, the anti-foundationalist arguments of these thinkers found new relevance in the explosion of structuralist and post-structuralist theory which reverberated through American literature departments in the 1970s and 80s: "James and Dewey were not only waiting at the end of the dialectical road which analytic philosophy traveled, but are waiting at the end of the road which, for example, Foucault and Deleuze are currently travelling" (xviii). Of course, these two groups—pragmatists and post-structuralists—are frequently accused of purveying ideas that are both philosophically relativistic as well as politically dangerous or disabling, and Rorty has seen

his fair share of this criticism as well. To put it in a perhaps overly schematic way, his early, more philosophically-oriented work (which includes the two aforemen-
tioned volumes) can be said to concentrate on the former charge of relativism—an accusation, he maintains,
which has teeth only if one believes in an objective,
neutral language which stands outside of time and
place. His later work has been increasingly concerned
with engaging the political questions posed by a pragmatist outlook. As Rorty himself acknowledges, the
"most powerful" objection to pragmatism is the "con-
sequence" that:

> when the secret police come, when the tortur-
> ers violate the innocent, there is nothing to be
> said to them of the form "There is something
> within you which you are betraying. Though
> you embody the practices of a totalitarian
> society which will endure forever, there is
> something beyond those practices which con-
> demns you." (*Consequences* xlii)

In other words, if we do not have any transcendent,
foundational criteria for choosing between languages,
or world-views, how can we argue against, say, the
Nazis? Further, if one's political and moral vocabulary
is a contingent product of time and place, how can one
be motivated to defend the values of this vocabulary?

Rorty's book *Contingency, Irony, and Solidarity*,
published in 1989, can be viewed as a way of trying to
answer these questions. First of all, the book contends,
"the notions of criteria and choice...are no longer in

point when it comes to changes from one language game to another" for the simple reason that such criteria and choices may only be formulated in the terms of a specific language game (6). Instead, Rorty suggests, changes in vocabularies are more a result of the power of what he calls "redescription." Drawing upon Thomas Kuhn's accounts of how scientific revolutions occur, Rorty reminds us that Galilean mechanics did not supersede Aristotelian conceptions of the world because the former was the superior choice based upon a mutually acceptable set of criteria; instead, Galileo offered an entirely new set of criteria for intellectual inquiry which displaced those of Aristotle. Galileo re-described the world that had been previously described by Aristotle by offering a new language game which made the old language game look bad. Thus, Rorty concludes, "nothing can serve as a criticism of a final vocabulary save another such vocabulary; there is no answer to a redescription save a re-re-redescription" (80).

The sort of intellectual Rorty prefers, then, is one who makes herself familiar with as many vocabularies and language games as possible by acquainting herself with as many novels and ethnographies as she can get her hands on. In doing so, this intellectual becomes an "ironist" about her own vocabulary, recognizing it as a contingent product of the time and place in which she was born. Furthermore, Rorty asserts, in his desired post-metaphysical culture, "novels and ethnographies which sensitize one to the pain of those who do not speak our language must do the job which demonstrations of a common human nature were supposed to do" (94). That is, the job of building human solidarity.

Hence, we might be able to characterize Rorty's pragmatist response to the "Nazi question" as consisting of
two answers. First, one doesn't refute Nazis, or any
other world-view; one offers a redescription of the
world which makes their description look untenable.
Second, and Rorty is clear that this consists more of a
hope than a guarantee, the properly ironist intellectual,
with her wide range of acquaintance, will have read too
many novels and ethnographies to fall for a vocabulary
which imagines itself to have some privileged relationship to Truth, and which ignores the pain of others.

Yet Rorty also hesitates to claim too much for the
political uses of either redescription or ironist self-con-
sciousness. In fact, he notes that "redescription often
humiliates" (90); that is, the act of re-casting the world
in the terms of a new language game can often have
cruel consequences, as the one redescribing the world
overwhelms and makes irrelevant the descriptions and
language games upon which others had based their lives
(which, as Rorty explains, is what O'Brien does to
Winston Smith in *1984*, and what Humbert does to
Lolita in *Lolita*). Indeed, Rorty cautions that while the
desire to craft a new final vocabulary which redescribes
the world apart from the language games one inherited
is a central activity of ironist self-creation, it is also one
which is largely irrelevant to public life. Thus, he suggests that the ironist intellectual enact a kind of cognitive public/private split: that one's "radical and continuing doubts about [one's] final vocabulary" (72), and
the ensuing attempt to redescribe the world as an act of
self-creation, be kept private, while one's public life
remains dedicated to the liberal hope of diminishing

cruelty and expanding human solidarity. In short, Rorty's model intellectual is what he calls a liberal ironist: one who continues to defend and support principles of liberal hope, despite their lack of metaphysical guarantees, by "distinguish[ing] between redescription for private and for public purposes" (91).

This provocative suggestion for separating political and philosophical (or aesthetic) pursuits is also one of Rorty's most controversial, and in our interview he discusses his responses to some of the objections to this proposal. What is important to note here is the way this proposal highlights his insistence that political concerns take precedence over philosophical principles, and that, if anything, the latter should be tailored to fit the former. Indeed, as he puts it in the first volume of his Philosophical Papers (*Objectivity, Relativism, and Truth*) Rorty has long argued for "the priority of democracy to philosophy."

Thus, after helping to revive American pragmatism—a philosophy he describes as particularly suited to democratic politics—Rorty has turned in his most recent work to the more pressing concerns of those politics, particularly in *Achieving Our Country*. We hope that the following interview will further illuminate his most recent political interventions, and their relation to the larger body of his thought.

Derek Nystrom and Kent Puckett
September, 1998

TOWARDS A NEW OLD LEFT

Q: We'll start with an obvious question: Why did you write *Achieving Our Country*?

RR: In an inchoate way, I've always wanted to write something about the Left in America. I've been buying books more or less relevant to the subject—books on American radicalism at various stages in the nation's history—for years and years. I knew I'd like to write something about American intellectual history, but had no very definite plan. Then Harvard asked me to give the Massey lectures on American Civilization. I was delighted, because my hero Irving Howe had given them. I liked the idea of following in his footsteps. So I set aside a year to read some more, and to try to write something.

Q: In *Achieving Our Country* you make a spirited defense of being a Cold War liberal—that is, an anticommunist liberal—and I was wondering if you could expand on that a little bit, because you suggest that had the Reformist Left been stronger they could have crafted an anti-communism that wouldn't have been the horrible McCarthyite anti-communism. I was wondering if you could talk a little bit more about what that might have looked like.

RR: There was a non-McCarthyite kind of anti-communism. People like Dean Acheson thought of the communists in the same terms as people like Norman Thomas, or for that matter Senator Vandenberg. Before McCarthy, people like Martin Dies and J. Parnell Thomas had been trying to get what they could out of anti-communist hearings demagoguery, but they were disdained by many politicians of both parties. Then McCarthy somehow managed to get anti-communism front and center and scared the life out of everybody. He gave anti-communism a bad name.

Q: I guess the question would be, how would it have been possible—maybe if only rhetorically—to craft a strong anti-communist and a strong socialist worldview?

RR: What's the problem?

Q: I guess, where's the wiggle room, given a McCarthyite culture?

RR: Well, all kinds of people during McCarthy's peak **years were saying the same thing they had said before**

and after: that socialism was a good idea in some form or other, because unrestricted capitalism, like the man said, immiserates the proletariat. Unfortunately, they continued, socialism has been perverted by mad tyrants like Lenin and Stalin, who have erected an evil empire. So now you had to fight the evil empire with the one hand, and forge democratic socialism with the other. I don't see a lack of wiggle room. McCarthy and his people, of course, said that any suggestion that capitalism needed any improvement or correction was lending aid and sympathy to the evil empire. But, of course, that was not so.

Q: Why do you think that McCarthy was able to do for scurrilous right-wing anti-communism what people like Martin Dies couldn't do?

RR: I don't know. Perhaps he was slightly more unscrupulous. Why did Pat Robertson and Jerry Falwell suddenly make it big? How did they break out of the little world of the televangelists and into semi-control of the Republican party? I don't really know. Every once in a while fundamentalists and unscrupulous demagogues manage to break out of their cages and to whip the masses into a frenzy.

Q: Were you at Yale during this period?

RR: I was at Chicago until '52, and then I was at Yale from '52 to '56. I remember watching the Army-McCarthy hearings at Yale. Chicago was perhaps the Left-most American university except maybe CCNY and Columbia. When the communists took Czechoslovakia in '48, I was a member of the Chicago student senate (or whatever they called it). I introduced a resolution of sympathy with the students of Charles University who'd been killed by the communists. It was killed 40-2, because it was seen as lending aid and comfort to the capitalists. It was viewed as red-baiting. In those days, Chicago students genuinely believed that saying anything nasty about Stalin counted as red-baiting. The student newspaper was communist, and eventually it turned out that the editor had been registering for one credit a quarter. He was getting paid, believe it or not, by Moscow gold. He was being paid by the Party to run the student newspaper. When McCarthy came along and said the communists had infiltrated everywhere, he could produce lots of similar examples.

But, of course, Chicago was not typical of the American academy at that time. I spent my time at Chicago making red-baiting remarks, as I had been brought up to do. I became unpopular with my fellow students for making them.

Q: Is there necessarily a difference between what you call "Moscow gold" and the funding that the CIA provided to anti-communist groups like the Congress for Cultural Freedom during the Cold War?

RR: The difference is that Stalin's was a bad government and ours was a relatively good government. Also, when you took Stalin's money you worked to Stalin's orders; whereas when you took the CIA's money, you didn't really work to their orders. People like Stephen Spender and Melvin Lasky (the editors of *Encounter*) were supposed to have known where the money was coming from. Maybe they did. However, I don't think they were pressured to do anything; they just did what came naturally—and that was exactly what the CIA wanted them to do. I think Christopher Lasch's suggestion that the money from the CIA showed that Spender and Lasky were just as dirty as everybody else was wrong. The anti-communist intellectuals in Europe, whose writings were published with the help of CIA money, were heroic figures—people like Silone and Kuestler and Raymond Aron. Being anti-communist in the late 1940s in France was not easy. Aron got a really hard time. I think they were very good people, and I don't want their memories soiled forever by Lasch's association of them with the CIA.

Q: Your account of the Cold War in the new book is primarily about what the Cold War wasn't: that it wasn't, as you suggest the Cultural Left sometimes thinks, simply this monolithic, ideological scam invented by the government to keep us in line and to justify endless military spending. Could you talk a bit more about what you think the Cold War was about: what was the point, besides registering moral outrage with Stalin? And, if we're trying to reunite the Left afterwards, what are the things you think we could learn from the Cold War?

RR: I'm not sure there's anything particularly positive to be learned. There was a certain amount of unanimity under Truman. Big business, fat-cat Republicans, and the liberals I keep citing like Schlesinger, Galbraith, Eleanor Roosevelt and the like all agreed that the battle fought in World War II to make the world safe for democracy had to be continued because we had run up against another anti-democratic evil empire. We had to start in containing communism. I think they were right. Like any war, the Cold War turned into an occasion for six different kinds of corruption and deception. In the end, we got what had been the primary objective of the Cold War: a chance for democratic governments in Eastern Europe. But we also had memories of the assassination of Allende, of the Vietnam War, and other horrors. So like any other war, the Cold War left all kinds of ghastly things in its wake.

You can look at World War II as having had all kinds of secret agendas. (Why didn't we bomb the headquarters of I.G. Farben, for example?) But World War II didn't last long enough to generate its own internal corruptions, so it can be remembered as a fairly straightforward crusade. I think about half the Cold War can be remembered as a fairly straightforward crusade. The other half consisted of opportunistic and disastrous adventures by people like General Westmoreland and Henry Kissinger. But the Cold War doesn't strike me as having a great big overall meaning. It was just the usual mess that any war is.

Q: Through much of *Achieving Our Country*, you discuss the New Left, and while you do qualify these discussions by arguing that there were a lot of important things the New Left did, because the Old Left wasn't able to fight the battles that the New Left needed to fight—to stop the Vietnam War, to push civil rights agendas, etc.—there does seem to be a kind of Decline and Fall narrative. You seem to claim that, until the '60s, the Reformist Left was doing the right thing, but around the '60s, things started to fall apart. The intellectual Left lost its connection with the labor movement, and stopped worrying so much about money and started worrying about stigma, as you put it. One of my questions is why you cite the break between Left intellectuals and labor here. Others, such as Kim Moody, have suggested that in fact it was the Red Scare and purges in the CIO that forced a lot of Left-aligned intellectuals out of a close, on-the-ground connection with the labor movement. In other words, the break between the Left and labor, and between intellectuals and labor, was in the late '40s and early '50s, rather than the '60s.

RR: That doesn't make sense to me.

Q: Well, people like Moody argue that a lot of the people who were arguing for a more aggressive "social unionism" were victims of purges in the CIO, and what was left were people who were more amenable to a kind of "business unionism," to a kind of narrowing of the union agenda to contracts, as opposed to being part of a larger social democratic movement.

RR: Some of that may be true, but I'm not sure how many such people there were. Certainly some people— people left over from the '30s who had thought the united front was a good idea—were loath to give up the wartime alliance with the Communists. Reuther and Lewis and others did a good job of getting rid of the communists. They may have taken some non-communist social activists out with them, but I'd be surprised if there were very many.

Q: The argument on this version of the story, though, is that this is where the tremendous advances that the Left made in the '30s and '40s were rolled back.

RR: I don't see that. If you thought that the US should have something like the British Labour Party, as opposed to the simply ad-hoc, pragmatic compromises that the steel, auto, and coal workers were making, then of course your expectations were disappointed. But I doubt it would have made much of a difference if we had had an analogue of the British Labour Party as opposed to union leaders like Hillman and Reuther having the influence they did within the Democratic Party. Moody's claim that once upon a time there was a great revolutionary spirit amongst the American working class and that it was betrayed by its leaders in the late '40s seems wrong. There was an attempt to get better wages and working conditions, and they got some of those things.

Q: Given your somewhat in-between generational location—as you describe in *Achieving Our Country*, you were raised in an Old Left family—how would you characterize your politics: Old Left, New Left, somewhere in-between?

RR: It seems to me just plain ordinary Old Leftism. Consider Michael Walzer, who's approximately my age, and was a student of Howe's at Brandeis. I think his take on contemporary politics and mine are pretty much identical. He and I thought of ourselves as on the Left both before the '60s and after the '60s, thought of the communists as a goddamned nuisance who had to be got rid of, and also thought of the far-out student radicals of the '60s as a nuisance we had to get rid of, lest they be used against the Left by the Right. Mine doesn't seem to me a very distinctive point of view—it's just plain ordinary Old Left.

Q: I guess I may be asking that biographically oriented question because it struck me, especially in that section of *Achieving Our Country* as well as in "Trotsky and the Wild Orchids" that your more recent political writing has also, it seems, been more biographically motivated.

RR: It's just a symptom of age...

Q: And your description of the Reformist Left circle in which you were raised seems to imply, "Why can't we go back to this?" One response might be that it may not be that easy any more—we can't just rely on an old New Deal politics, that the ground has moved out from under that in a certain way.

RR: I guess I just don't see what the change has been. What's wrong with New Deal politics?

Q: One would be tremendous demographic shifts— who makes up the working class now. Yes, in some ways, the New Deal was able to mobilize diverse elements of the working class, but it was almost all European "ethnics" who were organized, and now it's a lot more difficult to do that when you have a more multicultural working class.

RR: I don't see that. Why should the difference between the Poles, the Italians, and the Irish be thought of as less than the difference between the Vietnamese and the

Mexicans? Why are we supposed to be more multicultural now than we were in 1910? The Poles didn't much like the Irish, even though they had Catholicism in common. If you tell the Chinese and the Vietnamese that they have Buddhism in common, that doesn't diminish the diversity and the antagonism.

Q: On the other hand, in some accounts of the failure of the AFL-CIO, like Mike Davis' *Prisoners of the American Dream*, the idea isn't that multiculturalism is a new phenomenon, but rather that the AFL-CIO couldn't deal with or understand the rank-and-file multiculturalism they already had—that divisions between black laborers and white laborers...

RR: That isn't multiculturalism; it's straightforward racial prejudice. Why use the term "culture" for something like anti-semitism or racial segregation? The Old Left tried to get organized labor on the side of civil rights—to support the anti-poll tax, anti-lynching, and anti-segregation laws. With some unions they succeeded, with other unions they failed. It seems much the same nowadays.

THE NEW LEFT INTO A CULTURAL LEFT

Q: I'm interested by your take on the genealogy of the Cultural Left. One of the things that I got out of that film about the New York Intellectuals, "Arguing the World," is that members of the Old Left saw it as a major triumph that the *Partisan Review* was mixing cultural criticism with politics—that for people like Lionel

Trilling and Clement Greenberg, it was important that politics and culture be brought together.

RR: I don't think it was a major triumph. I think all that was important was that high culture ceased to be seen as an enemy of Leftist politics. People like Nicholas Murray Butler, the President of Columbia in the '20s, and President Lowell of Harvard wanted to use high culture to support social conservativism. They did not think Jews and radicals could have high culture. What Trilling, Howe et al. did was to take what we now call literary modernism and claim that *this* was high culture, and that it belonged to the Left. Actually, many great modernist writers were fascist, just as C.P. Snow said. But that didn't matter, as long as the study of the high culture of the day was associated with the Left rather than the Right. Bringing culture and politics together was something else. *Partisan Review* had two kinds of articles: questions on the relation between Pound and Eliot, and questions like "Shall we ally ourselves with the communists?" or "Should we break with the Trotskyites?" The two topics did not really have much to do with each other.

Q: I wonder in that case if we could see the *Partisan Review*, with its attention to both politics and culture, as participating in a kind of "politics of difference"? That is, were these New York Intellectuals trying to consolidate a cultural identity for themselves in a way familiar to academic or Cultural Leftism?

RR: I don't see the analogy. The politics of difference tends to emphasize the cultures of the oppressed. "You may not realize it, but the slaves after spending their sixteen hour day had this terrific culture going; the Chicanos, after their sixteen hour day had their terrific culture going." This kind of thing has nothing to do with the old *Partisan Review*, which typically made fun of the idea of proletarian culture. After they'd broken with the Communist Party they had no use for socialist realism, proletarian art, the culture of the oppressed, or anything of the sort. The group identity that they were interested in was the group of New York Intellectuals. For the first time in American history, there were Jewish intellectuals in America as there had been Jewish intellectuals in Germany. That was a big enough identity for them to set up.

Q: They were, though, intimately worried about how to connect culture with politics—a question that intellectuals seem to keep worrying about...

RR: Intellectuals only worry about that question if they've read enough Marxism to worry about the existence of things called "bourgeois ideals," "bourgeois ideology," "bourgeois culture," "bourgeois intellectuals," and so on. I think as Marx fades away, such worries may recede.

Q: One of the things I found most interesting in "Arguing the World" were the accounts that Nathan Glazer and Daniel Bell gave of how they felt when the students took over Columbia in '68; in some ways they were quite on their side and yet they were furious that the institution of the university was being attacked. I guess things were slightly different at Princeton, but I was wondering how your own institutional location affected the way you experienced that period.

RR: I can tell you one story. The night after the students had occupied Columbia there was a meeting of purportedly Left faculty in the house of a millionaire professor of history. We were all to discuss the question of why our students were so complacent—why hadn't they occupied Princeton's buildings? I thought this was the stupidest thing I had ever been asked. Obviously this guy had made a big mistake in asking me to the meeting. I managed to keep my mouth shut, because I was the only person there who thought they *shouldn't* occupy university buildings. Eventually some students did occupy the administration building. They were served coffee and donuts, and eventually went away.

The faculty at Princeton, like the faculty everywhere else, organized groups with names like "Faculty Against the War in Vietnam." I was their treasurer, or secretary, or something of the Princeton group. We would go to New York and march through Central Park and stuff like that. But most of us had no interest in the students taking over the university. Every once in a while the students would take over or barricade something—some center that was financed by the Defense Department, doing classified research—so we would go and bail them out. But it was just a series of ritual gestures. I think the reason why Princeton wasn't like Berkeley or Columbia was the absence of street people. If you weren't a university student or rich you simply couldn't afford to live in Princeton. Whereas Columbia and Berkeley were near places where people without money could live.

Q: Are you suggesting that this made the political questions there a little bit more vivid—that there was something more urgent about politics there?

RR: Every drop-out from college in the '60s had a motive for staying around the university, and being in on university life by taking part in student demonstrations. It was a culture, if you like, perhaps the most interesting political culture available. If you dropped out of school you just didn't leave Telegraph Avenue, or the Upper West Side, or wherever. Nobody knew who was a student and who wasn't, so so-called student protests were usually a mixture of students and former students.

Q: But the particular thing about the demonstrations at Columbia wasn't so much that people from the outside were coming into the university and threatening its authority, but that the university actively and perhaps wrongfully exerted its authority when they moved east into Morningside Park and began construction in Harlem without any consideration for anyone in that neighborhood. I wonder if you would see that as a case not of outsiders coming into the university setting, but of the university overstepping its bounds.

RR: No. The university was just doing what it had done forever. The radicals just looked for anything that would make the university look bad. The pretexts were trivial.

Q: There seemed to be two ways of looking at these events which are not necessarily contradictory. On the one hand, Bell and Glazer were telling the students that the university is one of the best institutions of democracy, don't attack that part of it. Critics such as Barbara Ehrenreich have written, though, that some of Bell and Glazer's anxiety could be seen as a kind of class anxiety—that the university was also the source of their middle-class authority, and by attacking the university, and claiming that the university is complicit in the war machine, the students were attacking the ground of Bell and Glazer's cultural authority.

RR: Sure. I don't think they should have attacked the cultural authority of the professors. It was hard-earned, well-earned authority. Those were the best allies the students had.

Q: A lot of people who were New Leftists claimed that Cultural Leftists have nothing to do with the New Left. I'm thinking here of Katha Pollitt's attack after the Sokal affair on Andrew Ross and the *Social Text* crowd, and her being quite upset that this is what passes for Leftism now.

RR: I agree with her.

Q: Yet in *Achieving Our Country* you seem to argue that the Cultural Left is of a piece with the New Left.

RR: I didn't mean to. The argument I wanted to make was that the Vietnam War, Watergate, and the loss of public confidence in the presidency and the government all conspired to move the student radicals into non-majoritarian politics. In other words, the Marxist claim that the system isn't reformable came together with the widespread post-Watergate feeling that the

American government is hopelessly corrupt. This made it very difficult for Leftists to think of themselves as American patriots, hoping to achieve their country. But unless the Left wraps itself in the flag, it hasn't got a chance of practicing a majoritarian politics. Before the '60s wrapping yourself in the flag when you did Leftist politics was as natural as breathing. But that became unnatural after the '60s.

Q: This is the certainly the sort of thing that with which many readers will take issue—this exhortation to patriotism.

RR: One of them already has, actually. I just got a galley of a review by Joel Rogers and Josh Cohen for *Lingua Franca* which says basically, "Who needs patriotism if you have moral principles?" My response is that moral principles are terrific in Ethics 101, but not as spurs to political action.

Q: Another of the fairly controversial arguments of the book is your suggestion that the Left drop Marxism and the vocabulary of Marxism. The first question I have is, what about "socialism"? Is that a term you want to get away from as well?

RR: Irving Howe asked, years ago, whether if we dropped that term would it make any difference to the policies we advocated. Let's not worry too much, he said, about whether we call ourselves socialists. I agree with Howe that socialism was the name chosen by the most important Leftist movements of the last 150 years. But now the term has become radically ambiguous, as demonstrated by the way the British Labour Party split over the nationalization clause. The old guard said: We can't call ourselves a socialist party and sing "The Red Flag" unless we're for nationalization. Blair and Kinnock said yes, we can. Howe was, in effect, saying yes, we can. And if you don't want to call it socialism, don't call it socialism. Don't get hung up on whether it's socialism or not.

Q: One of my concerns is that I don't know how we can drop Marxism without dropping a lot of writing that we would want to hold onto, especially certain kinds of dissident Marxisms that have been really useful in trying to think of how we might build something like a socialist or a social democratic movement.

RR: Like what?

Q: Like Gramsci. There'd be a weird kind of repression involved if we just said, let's talk about Gramsci without ever mentioning the fact that he was a Marxist.

RR: Liberal protestants can still quote fanatics like Luther with a perfectly good conscience. I don't see why social democrats can't quote Gramsci, or for that matter Marx, with a perfectly good conscience. But it seems to me the kind of Leftist who says we must never desert Marx cares more about his own authenticity than about what might be done. Loyalty to Marx has become a fetish.

Q: In some places you've criticized Marxist thinking for becoming too much like a science, like Althusser's work, which claims to offer something totalizing, pure...

RR: I haven't the foggiest idea what Althusser meant by "science." His book seemed to me bullshit from beginning to end. I've got no conception of what turned people on in Althusser. There were a lot of people who found him important. But he completely baffles me.

Q: But even the people who aren't Althusserians—the people who say that what Marxism does is give us a science of society, a science of history—obviously that's one of the things that, as a good pragmatist, you would prefer we stop talking about.

RR: It would have been nice if we could have had a science of society or of history. But for the last couple of hundred years people have been building philosophies of history and social theories that turned out to be completely irrelevant to what eventually happened. Why keep it up?

Q: Is it worthwhile, though, to look to some of the analytic Marxists, or people who are interested in maintaining Marxism, but in a more pragmatic spirit? That is, to take a Marxist line of thought and turn it into something with which to make social policy. I'm thinking here of that series that Verso puts out, "Real Utopias," which includes works by Erik Olin Wright, and Joel Rogers and Josh Cohen. They're interesting in both cases because they seem to position themselves in a Marxist tradition, but offer local solutions to particular problems.

RR: Do you think they'd be any worse off if they didn't position themselves in a Marxist tradition?

Q: In a vacuum, no, but since they're speaking in a community of other politically minded people who identify themselves as Marxists, and who understand a Marxist vocabulary...

RR: Who are these people? Do people buy books published by Verso?

Q: Yeah.

RR: Maybe, but even if there are still ten thousand people who will continue to say, as Derrida says, "we must read and re-read Marx," they are fluff on the surface. It's an amiable exercise in nostalgia.

Q: Yet these texts, in particular, situate themselves in a policy context and are ostensibly marketing themselves both to humanities Marxists and political science types. There's some sense that in the crossover market, by having quotable bites of Marxist-influenced policy advice, they could actually influence public policy people.

RR: It seems a cheap thrill to have readers in both English and political science. Now if you had readers both in labor unions and in Congress...

Q: My main question, though, is what do you say to people who would argue that what Rorty is asking us to do is to repress a Marxist tradition.

RR: How about not repressing it, but taking it fairly lightly? You can argue that if it had not been for Marx, Engels and their friends, we wouldn't have gotten the welfare state. Bismarck wouldn't have been so scared,

Lloyd George wouldn't have been so scared, and so on. You can argue analogously that had it not been for Luther and Calvin we would still be buying indulgences. Both claims are probably true, but do you really want to bother about whether you're maintaining a Lutheran or a Calvinist tradition?

Q: So you see it as a ladder we have climbed so that it may be discarded afterwards?

RR: It's a ladder that is covered with filth because of the marks of the governments that have called themselves Marxists. You have two reasons for forgetting it. First, it's become a distraction. Second, it's acquired a bad name.

Q: On the other hand, though, you argue in the opening section of *Achieving Our Country* that, in the same way that a person needs dignity to understand themselves, so does a nation. And I thought of E.P. Thompson, who quit the Communist Party in 1956 when that made sense, but remained a Marxist—and that was a way for him to maintain his political dignity. I wonder what you'd say to people for whom Marxism is that language: the language of dignity and the politically humane. Is it worth maintaining it so as to be able to narrate your past, and thus to think effectively about the future?

RR: Perhaps it's important for Thompson's generation to hang on to Marx. I hope that the next generation doesn't have to. I don't see why this has to be passed along to our children.

THE POLITICS OF DIFFERENCE

Q: In the first chapter of *Achieving Our Country*, you described your desire to encourage Leftists to see our country as Whitman and Dewey did: as a community in which the state and social institutions existed only for the purpose of making new sorts of individuals possible. This sounds to me like a community devoted to encouraging difference, and the proliferation of difference, yet in other sections of the book you chastise the Cultural Left for relying on a politics of difference.

RR: That's because I'm thinking of individual difference rather than group difference. I don't care whether anybody thinks of themselves as Vietnamese-American, Italian-American, or Baptist. I would just like them to be free to make up their own lives, in a good Nietzschean manner.

Q: Bruce Robbins, in a recent article in *Public Culture* ("Sad Stories in the International Public Sphere: Richard Rorty on Culture and Human Rights"), offers an interesting description of culture and difference which may be useful here: "Culture signifies both membership and identity on the one hand, and a loose, relativized, self-problematizing relation to membership and identity on the other."

RR: In the ideal case it does...

Q: So you think that's only an ideal case?

RR: Well, it's a very hard balance to maintain.

Q: Yet in the more sophisticated versions of the politics of difference, the idea seems to be precisely that we do try to craft our own individual identities, but we do so because we're part of different communities.

RR: Often we just put the communities behind us. Going to college, growing up, or getting away from home, should leave people free to say: I used to be a Vietnamese-American, or a Baptist, but now I'm past all that. They don't *have* to say this, but I don't see why they should be expected to have any particular loyalty to such groups.

Q: But it's not just loyalty; it's that this is part of the blind impress...

RR: No, it isn't. The blind impress is your unconscious. Group identity is what your parents tell you about— what we Vietnamese suffered on the boats, for example, or what we Irish suffered before they took down the "No Irish Need Apply" signs. You can remember that suffering, or you can do your best to ignore it—it's up to you. Whatever a Left politics is, it shouldn't have views on which choice a person should make in that situation.

Q: But isn't this what the politics of difference is about—clearing a space for that kind of choice? Clearing a space for people to have an association with various kinds of group identities, and even if they are still going to call themselves Americans, that American identity doesn't get conglomerized into just one banal identity.

RR: It seems to me the politics of difference grows out

of the notion that there is something called the White Anglo-Saxon Male Heterosexist culture which was (a) a pretty lousy culture, and (b) has insisted that everyone become a member of it. I find this an unrecognizable description. It wasn't a bad culture at all. It had quite a lot of room for all kinds of religious and ethnic identities, associations, parades, things like that. The sense that there was this vast pressure for homogenization seems to me a real Leftist myth.

Q: So descriptions of, say, women in corporate America saying, I have to change the way I act as a woman, to conform to a masculinist corporate ethic...

RR: Oh, sure, that's perfectly true. When the Irish went to college in my father's generation, they had to wear the same clothes the WASPs wore. I just don't find this interestingly oppressive and homogenizing.

Suppose you have a rhetoric of letting people have as much space as possible for their individuality, but one which simply ignored groups. That, it seems to me, would do as much for women in corporations, or the Irish or the Vietnamese going to college, as any rhetoric that paid attention to groups.

I want to distinguish sharply between cultural differences and stigma. Women have always been oppressed by men, and gays by straights, but not because they have a distinctive feminine, or gay, culture. Oppression of groups is a matter of picking out a group by possession of some ineradicable stigma and then humiliating, enslaving, etc., members of that group. The problem for stigmatized groups is not to get their "culture" accepted, but to get the stigmatizers to stop thinking that lack of a penis, black skin, or whatever, is a shameful thing.

So it seems to me a mistake to put stigma and ethnicity in the same box—to blur the difference between them with the term "cultural diversity." America has done a good job of melting ethnicities together into shared citizenship—being Irish is no longer a stigma, and being Hispanic is ceasing to be. But it has done a very bad job of lifting the bar to black-white intermarriage, which seems to me the only way in which black-white relations are going to be improved. It has been no better or worse than any other country in its treatment of women, gays, and lesbians. But these groups don't need recognition of their "cultures"; they just need not to be pushed around.

Q: I'd like to get back to this idea that group identity is something one can either embrace or walk away from. In the Robbins article I mentioned earlier, he describes this situation a bit differently—that one's relationship to one's "culture" is going to be *both* identification and a questioning of this identification. For example, a person will identify herself as a black person, and yet have a whole bunch of issues about what counts as blackness. There will be many situations in which she would say, unproblematically, I'm a black person, but in a lot of others that's going to be problematized. And this isn't just something intellectuals do—this is something everybody does. So when we're talking about the politics of difference, we have to acknowledge that sophistication.

RR: Yeah, *if* we're talking about the politics of difference. But why *are* we talking about the politics of difference? I just don't see what was wrong with the politics of individuality, conjoined with the usual attempt to repeal this or that law, overcome this or that prejudice, and so on.

Q: The question is that if one opens up this rhetorical space you suggest, where individuality is central, how does one, outside of a politics of difference, narrate the story of affiliation, disaffiliation, connection, individuality? How do you get the dignity to call yourself an individual in the way that you'd like without coming to terms with this group identity first?

RR: By telling stories about how people walked away from their identification with this or that group—Emersonian type stories.

Q: But that story will be very particular in every case, so that though the happy ending is individuality, the narration itself necessitates a politics of difference.

RR: Why not narrate a politics of contempt for group difference, a glorification of individual difference?

Q: That space is available; the politics of difference says we don't have to be fixed, that you can be an individual and this group identity can be something you leave behind, but the shape of that story is one that will nevertheless evoke the earlier difference.

RR: Why is difference now such a big deal? We always knew there were Irish and Italians and Vietnamese and gays and what-not.

Q: I guess it's a recognition of the kind of trials people undergo in being able to achieve their identity. In the process by which you're going to get to the place you want, you have to have this dignity, you have to be able to narrate your story, which will involve telling the story of the group you're from, the specific things you had to overcome to become the individual you are; and that story is going to be inflected, marked—stained in some cases—by the group you come from...

RR: I don't see what you mean by "marked, inflected, and stained." You can't write your autobiography without mentioning the stigma you inherited, but the stigmas were somebody else's idea, not yours.

Q: But what about the very simple fact that, in the culture we live in, your group identity is marked, and your life chances are limited or expanded as a result of that identity, and that there's got to be some kind of gesture of recovery to say, I'm going to embrace this identity that I'm told I'm supposed to be ashamed of. This is a rather powerful tool towards achieving some kind of political and social equality.

RR: That's one tool among others. You can forget about it; you can embrace it; you can do various things in between. I guess what bothers me about the politics of difference is the suggestion that you have some duty to embrace it rather than forget about it.

I'd say, talk about prejudice rather than groups. Before we knew that there was an African-American culture, or a gay culture, or a female identity, we talked about blacks, gays, and women getting an unnecessarily hard time because people were prejudiced against them. I guess I'm not sure that discovering they've all got cultures, or encouraging them to have cultures, has added anything.

Q: Could one say that individual identities come from a self-fashioning out of various group identities, and that you cobble together the things from traditions that you like, and leave behind other things that you don't like, and continually maintain a "double consciousness" or ironic relationship to...

RR: Why *group* identities? Consider the heroine of Sinclair Lewis's *Main Street*, growing up in Sauk Center, carving an identity out of the books in the library. It isn't a bunch of other cultures—its just Keats, Baudelaire, and the like. I agree with the argument of David Bromwich's book, *Politics by What Means*. Bromwich says that in the old days our sense of ourselves was modeled on Sinclair Lewis's heroes and heroines, or Stendahl's young man from the provinces. We used individual models to create a self for ourselves. But now, for some reason, we are supposed to worry about this other thing—what culture do we come from? What is our relation to that culture?

Q: What about the model of Stephen Daedalus at the end of *Portrait of the Artist as a Young Man*, or Ralph Ellison's narrator in *Invisible Man*—people who feel this tremendous push to embrace something they come from, and also transcend it and recreate it in a new way?

RR: Yeah, Joyce offers one model, but there are others.

Consider George Bernard Shaw, a contemporary of
Stephen Daedalus. Shaw wrote one play about Ireland
but for the rest of it, he was creating George Bernard
Shaw. He was quite aware of what the English had done
to the Irish as was Joyce or anybody else in Ireland. It
takes Daedaluses as well as Shaws to be sure, but I don't
really see that there's any particular reason to go one
way rather than the other. Some people are more like
Deadalus, some people are more like Shaw. Of course,
for a black American, it is awfully difficult to wrench
oneself out of the oppression of the blacks in America,
and simply be a free Parisian intellectual, though
Wright, Baldwin, and others did try it. Sometimes it
worked, and sometimes it didn't work—but it was
always hard. It was much easier for an Irishman
because the oppression wasn't as intense, the humilia-
tion wasn't as great. So, depending on just how beat up
you're likely to be qua member of the group, it is going
to be harder or easier for you to fashion yourself without reference to some group. But the people who don't
give a damn about the group are as intellectually and
morally responsible as the people who do give a damn
about the group.

Q: This discussion of the politics of difference reminds
me of the fact that, before you started talking about the
American Left in general, you focused pretty specifically
on feminism—you've written a number of articles
about feminism—and it seems to be a politics that
you're particularly attached to.

RR: One is always struck when one finds oneself guilty
of taking things for granted. I was raised phallogocen-

tric, homophobic, all the rest of it, and it took decades of propaganda to make me realize I'd been raised wrong. If I'd been raised in Europe between the wars, it probably would have taken decades of post-war propanganda to make me realize that they shouldn't have raised me to be an anti-semite. When you have the sense of your eyes being opened, you tend to write about how nice it is to have your eyes open. That's why I wrote about feminism. But it isn't that I think I have anything special to say about feminism.

Q: But there's been a particular interest of feminists in your work.

RR: Not much. There've been some angry replies, but I don't think any feminists have picked my stuff up and waved it as a banner.

Q: Except for Catherine MacKinnon.

RR: No. I just stole her stuff and wrote it up in a slight-ly different form. She hasn't used me, I've used her.

Q: I thought that at a certain point she had drawn on your anti-foundationalism for some of her work.

RR: She read me before I began writing about femi-nism, but I don't think it was a big deal for her.

Q: Is there a story behind when you decided to start writing about feminism, or is it a more gradual process?

RR: The influence of my wife, if anything—I suspect she was the principal stimulus. She began reading more and more feminist books. There were dozens of them lying around the house, so I began reading them. If I'd been single, God knows whether I would ever have read them.

THE CULTURAL LEFT
AND CONTEMPORARY POLITICS

Q: I wonder if your criticisms of the Cultural Left's "theoreticism," its need to theorize, is more of a philosophical objection than a political one. For your main critique of the Cultural Left seems to be that they are concerned more with "naming the system" than with crafting specific reforms. But I wonder if we can't see that this naming the system is similar to what the Right did from the '60s on. Sure, they had a whole bunch of policy positions, but they also concentrated a lot of energy on cultural strategy, on changing the terms of debate, changing the ground on which we argue about public policy. And this is perhaps what the Cultural Left is trying to do for the Reformist Left or with the Reformist Left, if anything—that naming the system may be a way of naming lousy vocabularies in which we're conducting our public conversations, and making some suggestions about new vocabularies or new conversations that would be more amenable to the kind of public policy decisions we would want to have happen.

RR: It's a nice idea, but I can't see what new vocabularies have been suggested. My feeling is that there's been a tacit collaboration between Right and Left in changing the subject from money to culture. If I were the Republican oligarchy, I would want a Left which spent all its time thinking about matters of group identity, rather than about wages and hours. I agree that the oligarchy managed to make the term "liberal" a bad word, and thus shifted the Democratic Party toward the center. It was a rhetorical triumph. The Left hasn't managed anything of the sort. What it has done is to capitalize on the success of the civil rights movement, and to get more and more breaks for various oppressed groups over the last twenty-five years. It seems to me that all the work of getting those breaks was done without notions of "culture." It was done using the kind of rhetoric Martin Luther King used, modified for the use of women, gays, and what not. King was not interested in African-American culture. He was interested in getting African-Americans the life-chances that whites always had.

Q: I guess we're disagreeing on what the term "culture" means. I guess when I say cultural strategy, I mean, for lack of a better term, an ideological strategy that presents a world view from which certain decisions can be made. Over the past 30 years, the Republicans have been very good at saying, instead of imagining the welfare state as this thing we have to ameliorate poverty, see it as an extension of Big Brother.

RR: I don't want to question the need for bringing a purer sense to the words of the tribe—changing the vocabulary used by the masses to describe this or that phenomenon. As you say the Republicans have been brilliantly successful at doing this. But I can't see it as an argument for the use of theory. Do the Republicans have a theory?

Q: I guess if you agree that this has been a successful strategy that the Right has employed, then we have to recognize that, to be vulgar about it, superstructural changes that the Right has enacted have in fact altered the economy, have shifted the way money works. Can't we argue, then, that there's room for a Cultural Left, which I would like to think could also work on that model?

RR: How about saying there's room for a rhetorical Left? But the question is: what rhetoric do you use? I think nothing is going to happen until you can get the masses to stop thinking of the bureaucrats as the enemy, and start thinking of the bosses as the enemy. I suspect this will only happen if there's a great, huge recession. But I don't see the Cultural Left as doing beans to bring about this shift in the masses' thinking.

Q: To take it from another angle, what about some of the impulses of the Cultural Left to seize upon this suspicion of bureaucrats as one that's not entirely misguided, and redirecting it towards a Left agenda as opposed to a right agenda?

RR: Foucault coming to the aid of Bob Dole? Watch out for the secret meshes of power?

Q: I don't know if we can see this as purely false consciousness if someone who is a welfare client finds the welfare state to be invasive as well as helpful. There's a certain way we can build upon this...

RR: Of course they find it invasive, but what do you expect?

Q: A less invasive welfare state? Why not draw from some of this populist fear of large bureaucratic structures and craft a less statist kind of Leftism that can still do the kinds of things that we want the welfare state to do?

RR: Does anybody know how to run a non-invasive welfare system? I don't think you can. You're just going to have to settle for lots and lots of Foucauldian webs of power, about as weblike and powerful as they always were, only run by the good guys instead of the bad guys.

Q: Without discounting the significant substantive disagreements between you and many on the Cultural Left, I keep wondering if it's possible that, to some significant degree, the conflict is the product of tone and rhetoric—that you dislike their revolutionary posturing, emphasis on righteous anger, and infatuation with theoretical language, and they dislike your casual, laidback and some would say even complacent tone. In addition, your rhetoric tends to be on the debunking, simplifying side, and theirs on the complexifying side. Do you think this is a significant part of it?

RR: Oh, yeah. I think so. Remember that I grew up redbaiting when red-baiting was unpopular. Because it was so unpopular, it was done in a sort of cynical, sarcastic tone. It's not a very pleasant tone, but I grew into it, and by the time I started in on this recent stuff it was the only tone I had. You could probably have a nicer and more effective tone, but it's too late for me.

Q: But how about the other side of this equation,

though? That perhaps if the Cultural Left didn't do all this posturing—which Robbins describes nicely as a reaction formation to their very political irrelevance...

RR: It's also just a plain ordinary power struggle within the academy for who gets the tenure slots. If you don't make a helluva lot of noise, the chance that any of your generation is going to get anywhere in the business is fairly small. So you have to exaggerate the importance of the difference between you and them, just as Howe's generation had to pretend that all things had become new when we became modern, that human nature really had changed in 1910, that literary modernism was a new birth of time—not really true, but useful for purposes of breaking into the system and getting a place in the sun.

Q: One of the significant differences between yourself and many on the Cultural Left is that your writing seems directed toward those who are, relatively speaking, powerful. The questions you ask often take the form of, "How should we residents of rich North Atlantic democracies, or we liberal intellectuals who have some cultural capital, act?" In other words, the concern is with how the powerful should act toward the less powerful. In contrast, a lot of Leftist cultural studies work seems to write from the other side of the equation—writing in solidarity with the less powerful. Whatever the pitfalls and shortcomings are of this position, it seems to result in a different kind of politics. In other words, you're going to end up with two very different kinds of politics, depending upon which audience you feel you are writing for. I was wondering if you could imagine writing an essay which is more concerned with arguing what the less powerful should do, not how the more powerful should act toward the less powerful. Is it possible to write with that kind of solidarity, or does it seem like a false kind of solidarity?

RR: Roosevelt said early in his first administration that, "If I were working for an hourly wage, I would join a labor union." This was a very important moment in the history of the labor movement. Was he speaking from the side of the less powerful? No. I could say to the janitors at the University of Virginia, for God's sake join a union. Would that be speaking from their side? No. But it's good advice anyway, even if it can be viewed as condescending.

This whole idea of solidarity with the oppressed on the part of the bourgeois intellectual strikes me as one of the many phony problems that we inherited from Marxism. John Stuart Mill didn't worry about whether he was solid with the women or the workers—he just gave his views. The Marxist trope of "Jones is just a bourgeois intellectual" never did anybody any good. It isn't something anybody should spend their time worrying about.

Q: And this is reflected in both *Achieving Our Country* and articles like "Two Cheers for Elitists," your review of Christopher Lasch's last book. In these places, you make an unabashed defence of top-down initiatives. But what about the idea that all knowledges are partial, imminent knowledges, and that the things you think should be done are in part a product of where you're speaking from?

RR: The masses always knew that. The intellectuals always knew that. Everybody's always taken this for granted. The first thing you say when you hear a political speech is something like "well, that's what it looks like to him." But I can't see that Foucault or anybody else has given us new insight into the tediously familiar fact that your views are usually a product of your circumstances.

Q: How can one acknowledge this point in one's writing and still say something useful, though?

RR: Why bother? Why not let my audience acknowledge it for me? Everybody knows that I'm an overpaid, privileged humanities professor. They knew it before they read my stuff. Why should I bother with self-flagellation?

Q: This reminds me of the labor conference at Columbia a few years back. It seemed to me that the point of that conference was to bring intellectuals in closer contact with the labor movement.

RR: No, I think the point was for Sweeney and the AFL-CIO to get some media attention—attention they need and deserve. The only way to bring intellectuals together with the labor movement is for the AFL-CIO to tell the professors, for example, that Senator Whosits has introduced a bill to change the NLRB rules for recognition of unions to incorporate the recommendations of the Duncan commission. That then gets the intellectuals to bang the drums, mention the Whosits Act every time they turn around, drag it into every conversation, and so on. That's about as much bringing the intellectuals together with the union workers as you are going to get. The intellectuals are supposed to give voice to desirable initiatives. In the past, they've given their voices to the repeal of the anti-sodomy laws and the equalization of male-female wages. So now let them give voice to the Whosits Act, because the NLRB is a mess. I don't really care about whether there's solidarity between these two social groups, as long as they are serving the same ends.

Q: What was your own sense of the conference?

RR: I'd agreed to give a paper in Colorado the second day of the conference. So I didn't see much of it. You got the tensions you would expect: between people like Joel Rogers who are out there getting people to run for school boards and city council, all involved in the nitty gritty, and people like me and Patricia Williams. We just stay in our studies and compose ever more effective little bits of rhetoric. The tension between Todd Gitlin and Robin Kelley was another thing. Kelley was not about to give up on group identity, and was furious at the suggestion that he switch from race to class.

Q: One of the things I found most interesting about Rogers' speech was his set of answers to the question, "What can intellectuals do for the labor movement?" Pretty much everything that came out of his mouth after that was, if you're a sociologist, or a political scientist, or a researcher in labor relations, here are things you can do. But the thing you don't want to do is deconstruct fairy tales, which is what they do in English departments.

RR: This review by Cohen and Rogers says, "He's just talking to humanities teachers," and I read that and thought, "Of course I am!" Who did they think I was talking to? Humanities teachers are people, too.

Q: Another point about the conference that you remarked on in *Achieving Our Country* was the booing of Orlando Patterson, and the way that pointed up a tension between different sides of the Left concerning what we should do in the age of global capitalism: do you keep borders open, or do you close them?

RR: Right. Do you save the working classes of the advanced old democracies by protectionism, or do you give up protectionism for the sake of the Third World? Do you try to keep the standard of living in the old democracies up in order to prevent a right-wing populist, fascist movement in the USA, or do you try to redistribute the wealth across national borders? You probably can't do both. I wish I knew how to resolve the dilemma, but I don't.

When I was a kid, I knew just what I would do in foreign and domestic policy if I were President. Nowadays I don't. I think this is a fairly widespread phenomenon. Forty years ago, you could believe that the U.S., through the U.N., could export democracy, squeeze the evil empire to death, create industrialization, and promote a rising standard of living throughout the world. I don't believe that anymore. It can't be done. How do you save the Asian economies without giving all the money to American and Japanese banks? I have no idea. Or consider Mexico. We in effect ruined the Mexican middle class by paying off American banks. There ought to be a way to avoid this, but I don't know what it is.

Q: The Columbia labor teach-in had been preceded, by a few months, by a labor struggle which caught the attention of a lot of academics: the Yale TA strike. I would be curious to hear your response to this event, especially given your comments about the relationship between labor and intellectuals, because this is one moment where the intellectuals *are* labor. Now as someone who has been in the academy for quite a long time now, I'm wondering what your reflections are on where we're going and what sort of things can be done to improve the state of higher education, to improve the state of the laborers in higher education: faculty, grad students, and other university workers.

RR: The adjuncts worry me a lot more than the TAs. I can't get really excited about how much money the TAs get. I can get upset about employing adjuncts. It seems to me that for the three or four years that you are a TA, the university says that in exchange for starving for these three or four years, you're getting a chance at a better career than you would have gotten if you had taken a job for real money. Maybe that's a fair trade. It's not a very conclusive argument, but it's an argument. I just don't have strong views one way or another. Adjuncts, on the other hand, seem to me quite capable of wrecking the system. You could de-professionalize higher education by hiring enough adjuncts. You could eliminate faculty control, take away the role of the universities as sanctuaries of the Left, as sanctuaries of tolerance...all the roles it has played in post-war America.

If you completely commodify academic labor you can get all the teaching done for roughly a third of what you can get it done for now. But I hope they don't completely commodify academic labor. It would proletarianize the faculty, and take away whatever cultural and political clout universities currently have.

Q: Wasn't it Dewey who helped found the AAUP? I wonder if there are other organizations that we need to invent to try to stem this tide?

RR: The AAUP is a really difficult topic, and somebody should write a history of it. It has less clout than it had before the '60s. In the '70s it went out on all kinds of limbs, and it left its membership way behind. The AAUP got in the hands of '60s radicals who staked it out in positions which lost it huge sections of its membership. I would love to bring the AAUP back to the power it once had, but I don't know how I'd do it. Bennington would have been inconceivable in the '50s. Now the university presidents are so contemptuous of the AAUP that they say "ah screw it, censure me." They really didn't say that then.

Q: But, getting back to your earlier point, one of the reasons why TAs are so angry is that we can no longer justify four years of starvation because of the rather uncertain promise of an academic job.

RR: The TAs who accept four years of starvation in exchange for a one in ten chance of getting a job usually have parental support. I think one reason why we get the graduate enrollments we do is simply the savings of the parents of the current crop. The next generation won't have those parental savings to draw on. So we won't have all these applicants for graduate study.

Q: That's one of the other things that worries a lot of us. The next generation of academics will only consist of people who had enough money for graduate school. So we won't have a next generation of working class scholars.

RR: The universities do have the chance to do something for economic equality. Eric Lott, Susan Fraiman, and Nelson Lichtenstein held a rally a while back for the non-academic employees at the University of Virginia. Sometime I want to write out a proposal that the faculties of the universities tie their own wages to those of the non-academic employees. The idea would be that you couldn't raise the faculty 3% and raise the non-academics only 1%, and you couldn't have a median wage for the staff that was less than half of the median for the faculty. There must be some such set of rules that you could institute. If such rules became a custom among the private universities, it would probably spread. The faculties of the big powerful state universities would say "I'm embarrassed to be teaching here at Berkeley where the ratio is 3 to 1 instead of 2 to 1, as it is at Harvard or Stanford." I'd like the universities to be a moral example. They'd be more of a moral example if they fixed it so that janitors with 20 years experience didn't get paid less than assistant professors than if they doubled the pay for TAs.

Q: Let's return for a moment to the stigma vs. money question, because this seems to be an important point in *Achieving Our Country*. The first obvious question is, can you imagine talking about both at the same time?

RR: Sure.

Q: So it's not as if what you're arguing for is that we stop talking about stigma.

RR: No, but we might divide our libidinal energy in half.

Q: Or even maybe not dividing it in half, but talking about both at the same time.

RR: See, that's the thing. Whenever I say this to Nancy Fraser, she says, "You don't seem to realize that questions of race and gender are inseparable from economic questions." I always reply, "Of course they're separable." For example, lots of white males don't get good enough jobs. So if you want a majoritarian politics then you may want to separate talk about the level of the minimum wage from talking about race and gender. The dream of the Left, particularly after Marxism seemed to have given us such a beautiful way of tying things together, is that we can integrate all of our concerns into a single consolidated vision. But usually we can't. We have to say one thing to one audience at one time and other things to other audiences at other times.

Q: One of the arguments that seems rather persuasive to me is that, given the racial composition of the working class and the poor, if white intellectuals interested in class are silent on race, or at least hold that these issues are separable, it will look like a class movement being crafted for white workers only. The danger is that blacks won't feel that they're part of the movement.

RR: And the danger of the academy's concentration on race and gender is that white workers think they are being neglected by the academy. So you're going to lose either way. The white workers *are* being neglected.

Q: The question is, some people argue that it is possible that we can do this, that we can talk about both at the same time.

RR: Fine, if you can do it, do it. But offhand, I don't know how to run the two together.

Q: It seems that that's what the recent work on whiteness studies is trying to do.

RR: What's that?

Q: This idea that you start talking about whiteness as a racial identity just like any other racial identity.

RR: [groans] God.

Q: Think about the quote from DuBois about the wages of whiteness —the idea that white workers were convinced that, while they were oppressed, they were still better off than the blacks. So they were encouraged not to align themselves with the blacks, because of the benefits derived from their white skin.

RR: That was what Gompers said about the Irish. It's an age-old technique: dividing the oppressed into hostile groups so they won't vote against you.

Q: Fred Pfeil has a piece called "Sympathy for the Devils: Notes on Some White Guys in the Ridiculous

Class War," and the interesting thing there is that he locates the absence of whites from these conversations in the same way that you do, and what he ends up saying is, let's try to understand why a militia politics happens. The idea is that there's some way that you can get to class through a more fully articulated discussion of race, because there's a way to talk about what it is that these people are missing, and what's offered in its place is the militias.

RR: Consider Clinton's last State of the Union Address: something for everybody, no overall integration of policy: just I propose this and I propose that. That's about as much integration as politics needs. I think of the intellectual Left as dominated by the notion that we need a theoretical understanding of our historical situation, a social theory which reveals the keys to the future development, and a strategy which integrates everything with everything. I just don't see the point. I don't see why there shouldn't be sixteen initiatives, each of which in one way or another might relieve some suffering, and no overall theoretical integration.

Q: It might be that some of this thinking is that the Left isn't quite sure what those initiatives should be, and that while the theorizing may occasionally become a fetish, it can also be a way of stepping back to one remove from the situation in order to get a clearer view, so we can then see what the more specific initiatives should be.

RR: It never worked before. Why should it work now?

Q: But what about the Marxist insight of taking a step

back from the economy and saying, the economy in a big way works this way, thus our specific local practices should be unionizing the workers and organizing them.

RR: It didn't take Marx for that. Cobbet knew that, I'm not sure that the Roman plebes didn't know that. I think the idea that Marx burst upon an astonished world with the thought that the rich were ripping off the poor is weird.

Q: But isn't it more than just the rich ripping off the poor? It's that it's being done in a certain way, so to stop it, we're going to have to address the certain way it's happening.

RR: But he didn't address it. He said that nothing could change without a total revolution, one which abolished private property, created new ideals to replace bourgeois freedom and bourgeois independence, and so on. The rhetoric was entirely one of "No piecemeal solutions." The Left got hooked on this no piecemeal solutions idea, and on the claim that if you do propose solutions they'd better be integrated in a general theoretical package. But most of the good has been done by piecemeal initiatives that came out of left field. Stonewall came out of left field. Selma came out of left field.

There's a new book coming out by Richard Posner, in which he talks about the difference between academic moralists and moral entrepreneurs. It's sort of a polemic against Dworkin and other Kantian moral philosophers. He distinguishes academic moralists, who have a moral theory which tells us that we must do so and so, from moral entrepreneurs, like Catherine MacKinnon. She is his paradigm of a moral entrepreneur. She doesn't have a theory—she has a polemic. Most of the good is done by opportunistic moral entrepreneurs, who have a very specific target, call attention to a very specific set of instances of unnecessary suffering. Later on the academic moralists and social theorists come along and tie everything up in a neat package. But this latter activity usually doesn't lead to political results.

Q: What about Habermas's fear that local solutions may clear up one kind of suffering while exacerbating another kind of suffering somewhere else?

RR: He's absolutely right. I think this will continue to happen until the end of time. All social initiatives have unforeseen, and often bad, side effects. The idea that you can step back and fix it so that your initiative won't interfere with anybody else's initiative is crazy. It's as crazy as the idea that someday the meshes of the webs of power will be less tight than they are now.

THE INTERNATIONAL

Q: You talk about ethnography and the novel as two genres of ironist liberal education or edification. And while the novels get talked about a lot, specific ethnographies rarely come up: how has the ethnographic tradition in anthropology influenced you?

RR: Think of ethnography as being done by historians

as well as by anthropologists. Talk about the culture of the Socratic Circle, of the Roman Republic, of the Renaissance city-state. These are just as good ethnographies as those of the Trobriands. Before they invented anthropology, we were getting all the benefits of ethnography. When I mentioned ethnography, it was in the context of a bazaar surrounded by private clubs, an image I used in a reply to Geertz. Suppose that became the model for a global society. There would still be some people who would always be trying to become members of the club on the other side of the bazaar. Those would be the intellectually curious people who read novels, history, and anthropology. There would be other people without such curiosity. I still think of a bazaar surrounded by private clubs as a good model for a global civilization. But with luck, the clubs would have some exchange memberships.

Q: Do we, following Bruce Robbins, need more than "sad sentimental stories" for a genuine international politics?

RR: Genuine international politics would mean working toward a democratic world government. We need the countries of the world to do what the American colonies did when they federated. It took a lot for the Quakers to overcome their hostility to the Catholics across the Mason-Dixon line. But they managed it. Same thing happened when Tito, after the war, enforced an end to ethnic cleansing. The Yugoslav federation worked for a while. One thing that makes federations work is a sad, sentimental story about past ethnic, racial, and national hostilities.

Q: Well, the thing that struck me about Robbins' article was that it emphasized NGOs as a crucial tool toward being able to develop a kind of a critical plurality of political positions. Instead of just having monocultures talking to each other, each nation is revealed to have all sorts of internal divisions that need to be played out.

RR: The stuff about NGOs in Robbins' article reminds me of Lasch's thing that I quoted in *Achieving Our Country* about wanting to declare a separate peace with our opposite numbers in the communist countries. No, we don't; we want to abolish the governments of those countries. We want a situation in which the next time a Milosevic tries it, there are so many blue helmets around the gangs can't get organized. We want a global federation so that the next time there's a Saddam Hussein, the American Congress doesn't decide to make war—the world parliament decides.

Q: This actually brings us to another point in Robbins' article about which I would like to hear what you have to say. He makes the claim that, on your model of the public/private split, the international sphere is private, while the public coincides with the nation-state.

RR: Why does he say the public coincides with the nation-state? Because I'm patriotic? All good liberal internationalists who are sentimental about the United States are also sentimental about the United Nations.

Q: I read an article recently by Ellen Meiksins Wood arguing that just because we have this rhetoric of globalization, it doesn't mean that the nation-state doesn't matter; it fact, it probably matters more. The nation-state is still there for people who are making the deals about where the international capital can go. It is more and more the proper site of class conflict now.

RR: If we don't do it at the nation-state level, it isn't going to be done at all.

THE MARGINS OF PHILOSOPHY

Q: Perhaps we might shift to more philosophically-oriented issues here. Can you remember what it was like not to be a pragmatist?

RR: I desperately wanted to be a Platonist—to become one with the One, to fuse myself with Christ or God or the Platonic form of the Good or something like that. Pragmatism was a reaction formation.

Q: When did you start to have doubts about this Platonic ideal?

RR: In my twenties. Remember I already had an M.A. in philosophy when I was twenty, so I had been in the business for quite a while.

Q: But unless my sense of your academic history is skewed, it seems like in the '50s and '60s, you were still writing fairly straightforward analytic philosophy.

RR: It wasn't quite like that. My first job was at Wellesley, where I realized that I had been badly educated for a career teaching philosophy in the U.S. Analytic philosophy was taking over. But my own graduate school, Yale, had blinded itself to this fact. So I didn't learn enough analytic philosophy. When I got to Wellesley, I found that all my colleagues had gone to Harvard, and were up to date not only with Quine but with Austin. So I threw myself into reading Quine, Wittgenstein, Austin—all the stuff my colleagues were talking about. I retooled myself so as to become an analytic philosopher.

Q: What kind of education did you get at Yale?

RR: It was entirely pre-analytic at Yale. They were the most reactionary of U.S. philosophy departments until quite recently. The department was put into receivership some years back, and started up again with a bunch of analytic philosophers. But in those days, if you wanted a career, it was the wrong place to study. Yale had offered me a fellowship, and Harvard hadn't, so I went to Yale. It was decisive for the kind of training I got. If I had gone to Harvard, my career would have been utterly different. So I had to quickly fix myself up during three years at Wellesley, and again during my first few years at Princeton. I tried desperately to find out what the hell my colleagues were talking about, to get in on the discussions, and so on. After a while, I began writing papers on philosophy of mind. That was because the one analytic philosopher I really cared for was Wilfrid Sellars, and his work was largely in that area. I think it would be accurate to say that up until 1963 or so, I wasn't doing analytic philosophy because I didn't know how. Then, because I couldn't have survived at Princeton any other way, I did my best to sound like all the other guys, at least for a while.

Q: And if I'm not mistaken, Princeton was something of a center for analytic philosophy in America?

RR: It still is—the top-ranked department. Number one. We used to get messages from Harvard saying "we're only number two—we try harder."

Q: However, many suggest that your work has shaken the dominance of analytic philosophy. Berel Lang wrote the following in 1990 about both your role as president of the Eastern Division of the American Philosophical Association during its 1979 convention, as well as the influence of your *Philosophy and the Mirror of Nature*, published in that same year: "It may be too much or even yet too early to claim that the landscape of American philosophy, institutionally but to an extent also substantively, would not be the same after the events of 1979; as with most stirrings in the history of ideas, Rorty's revisionism was undoubtedly symptomatic as well as causal. But there is no question that in the decade between 1979 and 1989 significant changes occurred in the profession of American philosophy— and that Rorty was and remains a central figure in this process."

RR: I think that's wrong. No big changes occurred, and I was never a central figure. 1979 looks big to Berel because the unreconstructed Yalies, the ones who hadn't retooled themselves were the center of the so-called pluralist movement. Their faction, made up of everybody in American philosophy who wasn't analytic, got a majority for their candidate for president of the Eastern Division of the APA. My sympathies were with him because he was the underdog, and the analytic establishment was being very arrogant. I was president that year, and I made a crucial parliamentary ruling in his favor. I've never been forgiven by the analytic philosophers for that. I've also never been liked or trusted by the pluralists. I managed to fall neatly between two stools.

Q: Lang does mention that you played the crucial role as mediator at the convention.

RR: I wasn't a mediator. I did encounter the leader of the analytic thugs, who said, "I have here the crucial membership documents, and I want you to throw out pluralist votes." I said, "Don't tell me what to do, goddamn it," and charged out, boiling mad. I though the analytic establishment was being overbearing and thuggish.

Q: It does seem though that 1979 was the year where the drift toward pragmatism that you'd been engaging in for the past seven years was suddenly in the spotlight.

RR: Nah.

Q: No?

RR: Remember *Philosophy and the Mirror of Nature* hadn't been published until late in 1979. People only started getting copies in 1980. Also, it got mostly bad reviews in all the philosophical journals, and it sold slowly at first. Very gradually, in the course of the '80s, people started to read it, and eventually it did gain a certain momentum. But there was no dramatic turn and no spotlight. My stuff was continuous with what a lot of people had been doing in various areas: Sellars, Putnam, and Davidson, for example. Since *Philosophy and the Mirror of Nature*, American analytic philosophy has gone on its merry way without any noticeable attention to any of this stuff. Sellars is still largely unread. I'm read mostly by people outside philosophy. Putnam is jeered at as someone who has gone soft.

Q: Maybe we could talk a little bit about how your audience started to widen, and reach the humanities people who wouldn't otherwise read what was going on in philosophy departments.

RR: Insofar as I've had an influence, it's been almost entirely on people outside of philosophy. I don't know why they read my book. I was glad they liked it.

Q: It seems that, just at the moment the deconstructive wave was crashing through American academies, you provided a homegrown post-foundationalism that you didn't have to be in a French department to hear about.

RR: Yeah, if you wanted non-foundational sounding stuff, mine was as good as any.

Q: Since you then moved on to become a professor of the humanities, rather than a philosophy professor, was it also your conscious decision to align yourself with literary theory?

RR: No, it was repulsion rather than attraction. That is, what I wanted was a job that was *not* in a philosophy department. I didn't care what kind of job it was, so long as I didn't have to go to any more philosophy department meetings. When Don Hirsch (who hired me at Virginia) called me up and asked, "Hey, do you want to be an English professor," I said I'd come if I could be a non-departmental university professor. I hadn't thought about moving in the direction of English. It was just that I got a call from the chair of an English department who needed somebody to teach philosophy to English graduate students.

Q: What is your position at Stanford going to be?

RR: Professor of Comparative Literature. When it comes to finding jobs, I have been always dependent on the kindness of professors of literature. In this case, the equivalent of Don Hirsch was Sepp Gumbrecht. When I was at Stanford in 1996-7, he invited me to come to his philosophy discussion group. Like all German scholars, he thinks American graduate students don't know enough about philosophy. (Compared to German students, of course, they don't.) He's in comparative literature, so the job he cooked up for me is as professor of comparative literature. But I'll still be teaching philosophy to literature students, just like I have been doing at UVa. I didn't care about the title. I suggested I be called Transitory Professor of Trendy Studies, but nobody liked the idea.

Q: It seems that it's not only the case that professors of literature were becoming more interested in your work, but that you were becoming more interested in writing about literature.

RR: This too was opportunistic. Just as I wouldn't have written *Achieving Our Country* if Harvard hadn't asked me to give the Massey lectures, I wouldn't have dared write about Orwell if Trinity College, Cambridge hadn't asked me to give the Clark lectures. The Clarks had to have some relation to literature. I was honored by the invitation and thought, "It can't be that hard."

Q: It seems to me that those sections on Nabokov and Orwell are among the most persuasive in *Contingency, Irony, and Solidarity*. Your arguments about cruelty and re-description are fleshed out really nicely in those chapters.

RR: I'm glad you think so. A lot of people thought that the book was just carelessly thrown together: essays on this and that. You never really know when you write a book whether the chapters are just one thing and then another thing, or whether there is some overall message that the reader can pick up on. If you're lucky, there is. The most devastating review came from Bernard Williams, one of the best analytic philosophers in the business. He trashed it, saying that the book had no unity, that it was just a mess. A lot of people didn't see any point, or any unity.

THE FOUNDATIONS OF ANTI-FOUNDATIONALISM

Q: Rogers and Cohen, among others, have suggested that you have a dismissive attitude toward the sort of absolutist beliefs with which a lot of Leftist movements have generated strength: the use of Christianity in the civil rights movement, and so on. How would you respond?

RR: The next book I wrote after *Contingency* came out in German and French. It was called *Hope Instead of Knowledge.* It was supposed to be a reply to that kind of criticism. I argued that if you have hope, it didn't really matter whether you believe that Christ was the son of God, or that there are universal human rights. The essential thing is to dream of a better world. Hope doesn't require justification, cognitive status, foundations, or anything else.

Q: I wonder in that case how one would practice pragmatism politically, especially considering the number of Americans still influenced by religion. I heard Cornel West once talk about how something like 95% of Americans believe in God, and 85% believe that God loves them. That being the case: does the pragmatist try to mobilize these kinds of belief in, I guess, a Leninist way?

RR: Whatever works: Cornel talks Christian; other people talk Marxist; I talk pragmatist. I don't think it much matters as long as we have the same hopes. I don't think it's inauthentic to talk Christian, or to talk Marxist. You use whatever phrases the audience learned when growing up, and you apply them to the objects at hand.

Q: Some people would say, though, that without something like the belief in the Church, the civil rights movement couldn't have happened.

RR: Maybe so. I don't know. Religion is less important now than 100 years ago. The tide of faith has ebbed. Lots of people are commonsensically secular in a way that their ancestors couldn't have been commonsensically secular. I certainly don't think we have to get back to Christianity, or Marxism, or any other absolutist view in order to get anything political done.

Q: It struck me that the gay liberation movement stands as a movement that didn't have a religious or absolutist base.

RR: Yeah, the message was just "leave us alone." Not because we are X, or you are Y, or the world is Z. Just get off our backs.

Q: I wonder again about when Cornel West "talks Christian": when you mobilize that kind of language for political purposes, are you maintaining a kind of anti-foundationalist position while encouraging a foundationalism in others.

RR: Well, this is where the private/public distinction comes in. I think that the shared hope is public and the Weltanschauung justification in the background can stay private. John Rawls says that in a pluralistic society everyone has their own notion of the meaning of life, but it doesn't get in the way of politics because they agree to keep it out of the public sphere. That seems a good idea.

THE SOKAL AFFAIR

Q: Speaking of controversies over foundationalism, what was your response to the Sokal Affair?

RR: I wrote a reply to Stephen Weinberg's piece. Weinberg had an article in the *New York Review of Books* on the Sokal affair, which was divided into two halves. The first part said "anybody like the editors of *Social Text* who are so illiterate about science as to publish this nonsense ought to at least know they're illiterate. They ought at least to have some humility." That was absolutely right. The second part was a polemic against Kuhn and all his ilk on the grounds that physicists knew their own relation to reality, and Kuhn didn't. It amounted to saying "for any given discipline, you don't need a philosophical discussion of the relation of this discipline to the rest of the universe because the members of the discipline know the answers to all of the philosophical questions that could be asked about that discipline." I wrote a polemic, saying that Kuhn could be right or Kuhn could be wrong, we pragmatists could be right or wrong, but qua physicists, Weinberg and his colleagues had no special insight into the matter. We philosophers have our own questions, topics, answers, arguments. Knowing zilch about those, Weinberg shouldn't get into an argument with Kuhn, even though he was right about *Social Text*.

Q: Is this a sign of scientists feeling like the philosophical rug is being pulled out from under them?

RR: Yeah, like the priests, they like to think they have a privileged relation to reality. I doubt they do, but one might expect that they would resent it if told they don't. When the priests of the 19th century were told by practitioners of philological higher criticism of the Bible that they were in the service of middle-eastern creation myths, they didn't like it. In the middle of this century, the physicists didn't like it when Kuhn told them they were just trying to solve puzzles.

PUBLIC AND PRIVATE

Q: Let's close on a few questions that have been raised by the public/private split you have suggested. A lot has been written about the private/public split in the ten years since you first articulated that position in *Contingency, Irony, and Solidarity*. It might be nice to have you now, ten years down the line, offer any clarifications that you would like to emphasize.

RR: The original misinterpretation came from Nancy Fraser, who said "Rorty didn't realize the personal is the political." I think she and I were at cross purposes. I was thinking of one sense of private, something like Whitehead's definition of religion: "what you do with your solitude." Fraser was thinking of the private as the kitchen or bedroom, as opposed to the marketplace and the office. There was no relevance to what I was saying.

Q: I can understand keeping your will toward self-creation private if you're Nietzsche—in fact, I'd recommend it. On the other hand, take someone like Whitman, whom you discuss in *Achieving Our Country*: Whitman's will toward self-creation involved other people, affected other people, and you acknowledge that it had its influence finally. What do you say to the person whose sense of poetic self-creation requires other people and the opportunity for public transformation?

RR: I would tell her to go into politics. I didn't say everybody had a public/private split, but some people do. There is a spectrum here. Some people have no public consciousness. This is the case of the sociopath; he simply doesn't think that there are any moral subjects out there. There are also a lot of other solitaries: hermetic poets who don't care if they have an audience. At the other extreme, there are people who have a minimal inner life. Their happiness consists entirely of being the soccer coach, or being the pater familias, or being chair of the Rotary Club. My public/private distinction wasn't an explanation of what every human life is like. I was, instead, urging that there was nothing wrong with letting people divide their lives along the private/public line. We don't have a moral responsibility to bring the two together. It was a negative point, not a positive recommendation about how everybody should behave.

Q: A therapeutic point.

RR: Right. Recently, I wrote a couple of articles on a pragmatist philosophy of religion. I agree with James that there needn't be a conflict between science and religion because they serve different ends. They needn't cross. Metaphysics was the place where they crossed, and so much the worse for metaphysics. It's essentially the same argument as in *Contingency*: we contain copresent but distinct sets of equally coherent sets of desires. These may not always be able to be made coherent with one another, but they may not be any the worse for that. Plato was wrong: you don't have to get everything to get together.

Q: And what would you say to criticisms that your ironism means a kind of sneering at earnest liberals who don't want to acknowledge the contingency of their own values?

RR: That was certainly the way it came across. But what I wanted to say was: take yourself with some lightness. Be aware of yourself as at the mercy of the contingencies of your upbringing and your culture and your environment. I thought of it myself as offering advice rather than insults. My liberal ironist doesn't go around being ironic to everybody she meets. She saves the irony for herself. The liberal part is public and the irony part is private.

Q: But regarding this suggested split, Simon Critchley asks: "how can one be a Nietzschean ironist in the private sphere, which would mean understanding liberal principles of tolerance and abhorrence of cruelty as symptoms of *ressentiment*, and a liberal in the public sphere, where one would respect and act on those principles? Does not the public/private distinction of the self into ironist and liberal yield an impossible psychological *bi-cameralism* which would be a recipe for political cynicism (Nietzsche working behind a Millian mask)?"

RR: Well, I think James was just as ironic as Nietzsche, and as committed to having his own religious experiences—quite independent of politics, his family, or anything else. But he didn't think liberal sentiments were manifestations of resentment. Had he read Nietzsche he would have said, "yeah, Nietzsche is right about perspectivism, but wrong about liberalism." That is my view of Nietzsche. You can take over a lot of Nietzsche's stuff about self-creation without thinking that people who aren't interested in self-creation, or aren't up to it, are base—to be neglected or enslaved. An ideal Jamesian democracy would have a place for all the vibrant self-creating activities that anybody would ever want to engage in, but would not insist that anybody be self-creative if they don't feel like it. There's a real difference from Nietzsche there.

Q: One of the things that makes people nervous is when you suggest that one's pleasure in life is relegated to the private sphere. The public sphere is just for making sure everybody's free and equal, and the private sphere is where you actually get to have fun. And I think a lot of people want to talk about the public sphere as a place where certain kinds of self-actualization happen.

RR: I don't think anything I've said implies that self-actualization only happens in private. Some people take no pleasure in other people—only in their own solitude. Some people do the reverse. Most of us are in between. That's the spectrum I was talking about earlier.

Q: As part of your argument for the public/private split, you argue that the last conceptual revolution in political thought we will need was J.S. Mill. Is that the best thing we can hope for in a political philosophy?

RR: I just can't think of anything I learned from post-Mill writings that added much. It's just a report on my own reading, or maybe a little more than that. There is a book by Bernard Yack called *The Longing for Total Revolution*. One good thing about Mill is that he doesn't have that longing. The longing was the product of specifically neo-Kantian strains of thought. These didn't reach England, at least enough to affect Mill. As soon as you think that total reconceptualizations are necessary for political thinking, you've already separated from reformist politics and are on your way toward Leninism.

Q: What do you say to enemies of the welfare state who would use Mill to argue that the government stay out of the way of the private sphere?

RR: Did Mill say that? I don't think there's anything in *On Liberty* to lend comfort to the enemies of the welfare state.

Q: It seems to me that enemies of the welfare state have long used arguments about the private sphere to prohibit government intervention in the economy. Perhaps this is just a realm where we spend our time arguing about what counts as public and private and that's one of the many arguments that happen in the political sphere.

RR: Suppose Marx had never lived, and we all had to get

along with Mill. The Republicans and the Thatcherites would have been saying "the danger to liberty is the government." The Left would have been saying "the danger to liberty is the bosses, oligarchies, corporations, whatnot." They both would have had a point. But I don't see anything in Mill that would have swung him toward the one side or toward the other.

I'll tell you one line you could use for a title which I intend to use as a blurb for some book sometime. Richard Posner has always said that philosophically I'm on the right track, it's just that I had no sense of concrete economics or socioeconomic policy: "Rorty is still talking about 'oligarchy' and 'the bosses.'" I want to use that.■

Prickly Pear Pamphlets

The First Series